A NEW OWL BIBLE STORY BOOK

AF576695

The good friends

Illustrated by Gordon Stowell

Scripture Union

47 Marylebone Lane, London W1M 6AX, England.

Christian Literature Crusade

Fort Washington, Pennsylvania 19034, U.S.A.

First published in this form 1977. © Scripture Union and Gordon Stowell

This man was ill.
All day long he lay
on his back.
He could not walk.

Some friends rushed in
to see him.
'Jesus is in the town,'
they said.

His friends picked up
his mattress
and carried him to Jesus.

The house was full of
people listening to Jesus.
The friends could not
get in through the door.

So they climbed up the stairs

to the flat roof.

The roof was made of mud and wood.

The friends quickly dug a hole in it.

Then they lowered the man through the hole.
Everyone was very surprised.

Jesus loved the man
and wanted him to walk.
He said, 'Pick up your
mattress and go home.'

Jesus made the man well again.
He was very happy and so were his friends.

Jesus
loves us, too.
He knows
what we need.

You can find this story in Luke Chapter 5, verses 17 to 26